Unselected
Poems

**Unselected
Poems**
WN Herbert

Smokestack Books

School Farm
Lead Lane
Nether Silton
North Yorkshire
YO7 2JZ

e-mail: info@smokestack-books.co.uk

www.smokestack-books.co.uk

Poems copyright
W.N Herbert, 2024,
all rights reserved.

ISBN 9781739473402

Smokestack Books
is represented by
Inpress Ltd

Contents

Afterself	11
from On Your Nerve	
Why Stick Things Together That Are Happy Broken Up?	17
Imagine There Are No Actors	19
'I first became acquainted with Frank'	21
The Thoughtcafé	22
'I carried this café around in my head'	23
Now Imagine You're in a Theatre in Glasgow	24
'Too hip for the squares'	26
I Am Another City	28
In the Middle of Living	30
The Working Self	33
Homage to the Anxious City	
Homage to Catalan as Though It Were an Ex-Lover	39
Homage to the Rain Dissolving my Consciousness into	
Chocolate	40
Chorus of the Militant Food Technicians	41
Homage to Picasso the Inquisitor of Rain	42
Vision and Prophecy of Newcastle Yet to Come	43
Homage to Jamon	44
Chorus of Skin and Screaming	46
Homage to the Siesta of the Moustaches	47
Homage to Lampshades	49
Lament for the Improvements of Modernist Newcastle	50
The Revenant	53
neareast	
Afterwards	57
An Approach to Sofia	58
Ghost Guests	59
Hram-Pametnik Aleksander Nevski	60
Dvoyanka	62
Red Lullaby	63
A Double Blessing	64

Portrait of an Informationist	67
Murder Bear	
The Four Bears	73
A Night Story	74
Murder Bear and the Makie-Up People	76
A Murderous Sestina	77
from Murder Bear's Address to the Polar Explorers	79
The Passionate Psychobear to His Love	81
Bear Grills Bear Grylls	82
Hellbeareen	83
Hendecakillabics for the Restive Season	84
Didst Thou Ever See Murder Bear?	86
Murder Bear Has the Last Words	87
Murdered Sonnet	89
Montaigne and the Three Murder Bears	90
Ours Meurtrière dans le Métro	91
Dear Reader	94
Zeichentrickbärendämmerung	95
Little Instruments of Apprehension	99
Don Juan's Pilgrimage	105
Little Red Robot (Hidden Track)	134
Acknowledgements	136

Afterself

I know that I'm still in there, in
that fading frame. I almost hear
the final pop of synapses,
that old and faithful circuitry.
I know that I still have to die
in there to make the leap to here
complete in these new rituals' terms:
electro-resurrection to
continued, altered life. And though
the shift was seamless, just a switch
which woke me up forever, I
can't bring this afterself to think
of that familiar flesh as 'him'.
And so I sit outside me, watch
my body go: that flicker in
those eyes I've never seen like this
is me, now learning how to die –
a thing I'll never have to do –
and understanding what this more
than mirror feels about it. They say
the tear-ducts come online in time
to mourn. Although I shouldn't test
me yet I find I'm feeling for
those more elusive traces as
I hold the outside of that hand –
more soft, more creased – that I held with.
I'm feeling for sensations that
I know they can't yet duplicate:

The walk around the cold night block
that I took with my mother as
my grandfather was dying – how
we talked, though I was ten. I've lost
that frisson of familiar shock
to count again how young she was.
And that guitar book that I left
on the park bench, to show my first
girlfriend the girl who gave me it
meant nothing – nothing's left of my
disgust at sloth disguised as pride.
That woman lying in the grass
of our first garden, windfall fruit
rotting around her, with one more
button undone than necessary.
The student nurse in that shared house
who asked me to make her a dress
from black bin-liners. Something has gone
from those distended seconds when
the doctor's search for a foetal heart-beat turned
to something dogged. Something, I know,
should touch me knowing, decades on,
the child was more important than
the marriage. Then, outlasting all
our hate, regret filled up the years
which followed, till that instant when
my wife's death stopped all rage – that point
once snapped me like a filament.

It's true: I know when we look out
the window at the same time for
the only time, I do not share
a need to name that colour caught
between the names, the one that coats
the underside of all those clouds.
In five years' time they'll synthesize
these finer shades we cannot share.
By then I'll be resigned to an
eternity without myself:
twin to a temporary soul,
the copy will become a life,
without this relevance of touch,
its memories receding like
a galaxy, no faster than
the power of our telescopes
to catch it up. Until the thing
we thought was worth preserving is
as random a beginning as
the notion of a heaven was –
our limiting infinity
to how we wanted to remain.
We can't explain the microbe's need
to reproduce by citing God,
and to survive our deaths is not
to be ourselves. So this feels like
a goodbye that just won't be gone:
the final breath my last hello.

from
On Your Nerve

Why Stick Things Together That Are Happy Broken Up?

I spent those useless years
kicking the melody can
down an ingrained rumble
of the Dundee streets.

The weather in that dream
wanted to be everywhere,
but I made it confine
its activity to within

this city's traits.
Occasionally the cloud contained
a blue keyhole
for which I had no key.

Occasionally Frank's voice would ask
to be let out: he'd say,
'I was always ready to be
freed from the constraints

of any social being.
In fact I was so ready
I put the mirror on the fire
and dried my reflection.'

I had to be careful
I did nothing extraordinary
or comprehensible. That way
he wouldn't slip my tether

altogether: Frank'd say
'Nobody wants to sleep with
a white formless unit rising
and falling in the gaps

between paving stones.'
As a precaution I wrote
on my teeth instructions
as to how to cut the sky.

Then I'd squeeze his soul
like a squid into the space between
two panes of double glazing
but it wouldn't stay.

Now I've given up that ghost
it can only follow you home
tonight and on subways
with its inaudible charms.

Now I like the idea
of just having dirt in my pockets;
it's usually sugar,
but I prefer dirt.

It's ghost rain that's falling:
I walk for miles
through the cold sweating streets
and am still bone dry.

Imagine There Are No Actors

Imagine there are no actors here
                                      being really real
just you and me both
meaning it, or trying to
or hoping to find out by listening
to what our mouths are saying
just what it is we permit ourselves to feel.

Let's not for once get real
                                or worse, try getting even
about the innumerable invisible scars we carry:
aren't we real and/or odd enough
for company and comfort?
Let's just get complex:
something that actually covers the ground
between breath and thought.

Only 3 personalities in the US, Lowell reckoned,
and he should know, having the paranoid one
(that leaves us the hallucinator and the soap flake baby,
Baby) – people find it easier
being a type, leaving
the big stuff to your analyst.
Andy nearly got it right:
                                'I want to be a machine.'
Frank knew that
                the self's a gimmick
we can't help buying, like BLTs and half-caff lattes:
the in-persona this season is modelling
high anxiety with a plunging but non-smoking
                                            sensitivity,
beneath a dark splash of
                            aggressive but accessible

laddishness, finished with classic
inyerface hypochondria:
be it and enjoy.

Frank knew that
               a person's not himself
half the time, but buildings, others, alcohol;
circa fifty years of half-digested local history
and street maps, a city:
               je est une autre ville, as
Rimbaud might have put it
had he stuck at the day job:
               nothing flakier than
fucking off to Africa and trading arms
for your own gangrenous leg.
Nothing flakier, frankly,
than wanting to be real
               when it's your only given.

I first became acquainted with Frank O'Hara in the early eighties when I bought a copy of the Bill Berkson/Joe LeSueur *Homage* in the secondhand upstairs bit of a little bookshop in Oxford. The *Homage* alluded to these magnificent poems which had apparently blown the American minds collected therein, but it only quoted them in shrapnel-like fragments. So, at first, I had to imagine O'Hara into existence. The apparition I conjured up by this means proved so charming I went and ordered his books up in the Bodleian and that was that.

But there were all these blank pages scattered throughout the *Homage*. It was obviously a rejected copy, so another of my creative efforts centred around trying to imagine what was printed on those missing pages. This kind of space was so important to me then and is, I think, even more important now. When you're a nobody as far as poetry is concerned, unpublished and unnoticed, producing work that nobody seems willing to read, you need companions among the dead, and you need gaps in their biographies, spaces in their work in which you can insinuate yourself. And that's what those blank pages and those quotes from the poems gave me: they made Frank into an ideal ghost.

I would go and sit in a café called George's in the Covered Market and think about my dead. There'd be MacDiarmid and WS Graham (who wasn't even dead at the time), Valéry and Frank O'Hara. None of them would've got on with each other, but that didn't matter, because they weren't meeting each other, they were just sitting in an imaginary café in my mind talking into the air or writing or, like Valéry's M. Teste, doing absolutely nothing. I liked all those stories about cafés in Paris with Sartre at one table and Beckett at another and nobody saying a word. I liked the story about Carlyle meeting Ruskin and neither of them saying anything all night and Carlyle saying it was the most enjoyable evening he'd spent in some time.

The Thoughtcafé

I am sitting in a café sitting in a café
in my head with M. Teste, sipping what amounts to
a bidet of café noir, a steaming lavabo
in the bitter imaginary morning:
wherever we are I watch him never move,
his limbs and his moustache are limp and obedient,
his suit looks as though it's on a hanger.

M. Teste has control of the very seasons:
summer rain droops its eyelash over
the winter exterior, the hurriers are
confused for a moment in midst
of their hurrying. Their faces are red
from the cold and some of them
are annoyed by lampposts, so
the sudden materialisation of a warm *vespasienne*
fascinates them: one man kicks it in a dull clong
which is really a clock tower.

My hypocaustic sinuses fill
with cold noise as thoughtcafé and café
retreat, and M. Teste carefully
talks himself asleep.

I carried this café around in my head for a few years and there's a sense in which I've never left it. These days I'm working on a theory that the writer must be invisible, scarcely noticed at all by his or her culture or contemporaries, so that the work itself may have the greatest, most chaotic impact. I think that's sort of what happened with Frank even though he had such a big circle of friends. He never sought publication, he never made a big thing about his writing, and so no-one outside that circle noticed: as Joe LeSueur says in the *Homage*: 'I didn't realise right away that if you took poets as much for granted as you did breathing it might mean you felt it was as essential to your life.'

Anyway, I was also helping to run the University Poetry Society and one time we got Tom Raworth to come over from Cambridge and he gave this beautifully judged deadpan reading with hand-drawn diagrams and we all declared him to be our only epic poet and we had a great time as you sometimes do and next lunchtime we reconvened in George's and we ignored our hangovers. and we talked about O'Hara.

I mentioned I had this incomplete *Homage* and Tom said he had that book and his copy was incomplete too. So we compared pages as far as we could remember, and discovered perhaps even truly that we had each other's missing sections. We posted photocopies, and I carefully pasted mine in, aware that Frank had somehow placed Tom Raworth more firmly in my poetic landscape. The next summer Nancy Esposito brought me the *Collected Poems* back from New York and another freedom became purely imaginary.

Now Imagine You're in a Theatre in Glasgow

Imagine you're in a theatre in Glasgow.
Be perverse, pretend this isn't New York
in the 50s/60s; close your eyes: imagine
my voice is not 'a hick accent
a flat Massachusetts nasal twang'
pretend I amna Frank O'Hara if you can.
Go on, go on your nerve and fake it:
just for an instant think of yourself
as audience, primed for a medium none
of us expected in so gritty-glittery a space
as we're all really at: imagine a poem.
It's like the seconds after a car-crash
in which you know that's something gone
but you're still clinging to the normal road
seconds before: nostalgia has shrunk
to the instant in which
                        the enormity of your wound
becomes apparent. That's it, the zone
in which you can pretend
this is a theatre; that I'm not Frank
and you're an audience, so deft and able
I could say the sky was clouded with nipples
and you'd look up and wipe the splash of milk
from your unbelieving eye. You're smart enough,
that when I say a galleon is being put
through a pasta machine in the apartment
next door, you hear its groan. You're witty
enough to care about the speed and poise
and weight of words, that stuff you're left with
when you clear away the grunts and needles,
guns and fucks of real novels and imagine
a poem the size of a city, each line a street,
each word a cab with someone in it, carrying

their own silence in a case, cars cutting
across each other and honking out the thoughts
of other words, lying alone six floors up
and dreaming of a perfect haircut. Imagine
you're imagining a city the size of a poem,
the way it'd surge through stanzas like blocks,
interrupt the rhymes with briezy ads and weather.
Imagine visiting its bars and galleries and lofts
and cool down to a depth, a weight of blue
upon this city built of paper, gins, and voices;
the low glow of a fizzing set, piano on
the boxy dansette. That's it, you're home again,
sleeping in the wings of breaths in NYC:
you never left - how could you go to the theatre
tonight, knowing as you did that Frank's not here?

Too hip for the squares, too square for the hips, and I'm not talking about my trousers, or 'pants' as Frank would call them, as though an item of clothing were a passionate verb, as in 'I pant you pant we all pant for Frank's pants' which was, I believe, the intention, or, as he puts it in a cartoon collaboration with Joe Brainard, 'Red never gives back pants.' Joe Brainard always sounded like Brainiac out of Superman, and Metropolis was obviously New York, and Frank was therefore Superpoet, or that's how we viewed him, giggling over cartoons of gay cowboys and their pant fixations.

I'd like to say Frank O'Hara ruined five years of my life with giggling, but that was probably the dope; as Paul Morrissey said, you have no sense of humour if you're stoned: everything is funny. But certainly he ruined my writing with exactly that notion: everything is poetry if you're the poet. Actually, it was Allen Ginsberg who said that about Frank, but I believed him. It took me some years to discover my entire sensibility didn't agree: some things weren't poetry at all, like drinking too much and blethering and never revising, and some things were, like falling in love with language and staying faithful.

I was certainly in love with Frank's language; before there were any British editions of his poems I used to go to the Bodleian Library and copy them out of books into this dark blue journal. I got through *Lunch Poems* and most of *Meditations in an Emergency* before Nancy came back from New York with the huge *Collected*. That was a pretty Andy Warhol-meets-the-Venerable-Bede type of thing to do: be a copyist in the medieval sense so I could have these poems. I used to copy a few poems, write a few lines, then fall asleep in the library with my head in that big beautiful book and dream of a city that was half New York, half-Dundee. Did I mention I was drinking a lot at lunchtime?

No-one famous was ever there in the dream, just me looking into old junk/book shops and climbing on the monuments. But in Frank's poems the sky was raining names: names I didn't know like Larry Rivers, Bunny Lang, Joe LeSueur; names he loved like Patsy, Vincent, Mike.

I Am Another City

How can we be as fast
as alive as your glamorous
past we have to borrow
with our tourist eyes,

when what we know
comes so slow we take
years to be sure of it?
How can we answer back?

Some questions seem big
as Manhattan's accordion
buses, better to swerve past
and go on our nerve.

Except we'd expect more
of these, the charming
mouths of poets, if we stopped
to think about it, than

an echo of old brilliant
reckonings: the totality of day
ignored in memory of
Frank's feelings, the shadowing

eyes' rebound from the
luminosity. We'd expect us to
expatiate, negotiate
the depths of blue between

skyscrapers drowned in
our last century's certainties,
its bloated fifties, when
everyone was clear they were

quick, and thick in it:
louses in the luxuries, cock-
roaching the caviar,
reaming in the real.

Except, when we stop, if
we are the pause in which
space defines itself as
always more than questions,

we begin to know the shapes
replay themselves, the ways
of being are like cabs
yellowing up a street, always

the same, never the same.
These shapely vacancies left
by our brothers, those previous
others, like the memory of holding

someone's hips: that space
is where we are now, that
we've stopped to think
about it, within it.

In the Middle of Living

In the middle of living I found myself
in the Contact Lens Centre on Northumberland St.
It was 12.15 and I was wondering if
they would photo the back of my left
eyeball, that got me hospitalised in
Dumfies with a maybe tumour: you've got to
know the size of the wound, same way a
man's got to know his imitations, how
dirty is his Harry. Everybody carries it
in a blue case, among the lost papers of
unwritten lovers, unlived-with books.
You would have reached 70 by now,
a reasonable sweep of vision: ten years ago
you probably could have pulled me
back when I wrote poems of uncertain
sexuality, instead you died when I was five,
in the first summer of my deaths' arrival –
grandmother, great uncle – an ocean, a generation
off their coast. My dreams are in an
unreal city: Dundee as old New York,
a big sawdust-bare newsagents with
plywood counter, no papers, just the yellow
smell of news, ink in the lines of her hand
spelling her 'rock-depth of heavy trouble';
him climbing the hill past bespectacled pigeons,
mutton pie shops where cats went missing,
blue nudes in his heart attack pocket,
a bachelor before that had a second meaning,
his flat full of piano and the glimpse dissolving
at my mirrored self in focus without glasses for
the first time since five actually there
ageing into their faces, your voice, another city.

The Working Self

in memory of Martin Conway

the naked man with briefcase
descending three flights of lighthouse stairs
his neckmuscles held by a hatstand of stress
and a new version of the Inferno blackening his cerebellum
in which the only dead are his poetic texts
and those of all the writers he has ever loved
wanting to be asleep with all the fervour of the truly middle-aged
                is not
the naked man running into
the midnight sea at Teignmouth
with the surprisingly large-breasted girl
he will not sleep with later in the sand
all the car-load of friends all following The Wedding Present
from gig to gig all stoned and half-undressed and
sleepily Silenusian in the cold cupping sand
                is not
the student standing with a white-furred uvula in
the campanile of his newly-smoking throat
before the galvanised façade of Milan Cathedral
on his first morning in Italy, before visiting the Brera, the Uffizi,
focussing on the lens as it falls from his spectacles and smashes
on the delicious pasticceria icing of the paving stones
                is not
the seventeen-year-old staring at Rossetti's
loganberry compote of a dream of Dante and the corpse of Beatrice
remembering the final cold corner bust up by the bridge
by the Post Office where he stood for hours knowing
she would never feel the need to come back
not knowing that he would never speak to her again or know
her whereabouts or children or the moment of her death
                is not

the boy visiting a grandfather
he hadn't seen so long he had almost begun
to think of him as dead and dreamed about it endlessly
after the rapidly-following death
the slow hand touching the bandaged throat, the querulous
        witty voice
the dark conspiratorial spectacles, always
not dead after all or dead but still with him, murmuring
              is not
the boy who dreamt that all his classmates sat in darkness in
a circle and the circle was so large it seemed to contain
all the people of the multis at Trottick, all the people in Dundee
perhaps all the people in Scotland and in the centre was a figure,
cowled like a monk, rotating in the darkness with an index finger
pointing and revolving like a planet in an orrery
and when the figure pointed straight at him
woke up in the dark moon-streaked fourth floor bedroom for the
first time
              clearly alone

Homage to the Anxious City

Homage to Catalan as Though It Were an Ex Lover

It's like a language that you used to speak
quite fluently, but then you moved away
from the household of her hips, and as the weeks
rephrased as years you couldn't understand,
the patois of that profile and those hands
began to slip until you couldn't read
her in the phrases of those other throats
who conjugated you in warmer beds.
You realized that you no longer dreamt
in the sharp vowels of her breast and hair;
the names of her mind's streets had all turned gray
and you could only speak a dialect
which let you say you loved her all the more
though in the wrong case, and the perfect tense.

Homage to the Rain Dissolving my Consciousness into Chocolate

In the *continuitat* of darkened, rain-dogged streets
I follow the *carrers* with coils of wire dangling from iron balconies
and poems written on the tiles that name them,
the brick dust runnelling and palm-trunk cropping alleys,
the yellow cement mixer churning and
graffiti figure begging for one euro *carrers*.

I flow through the streets filling with *farmacias'* blinking signs
as though the raindrops are plugged with hypochondria;
I rest in puddles by the restaurant window
filled with blue glove puppets holding
banners that may be demanding 'Cleaner Hands Now!'

and I fill up the suggestion box for the Chocolate Museum
with requests for chocolate dogs! Chocolate batteries!
Chocolate abstractions! Justice chocolate!
The chocolate of austere beauty! Chocolate ennui!

Chorus of the Militant Food Technicians

Barricade the supermarkets of Byker & Wallsend!
Starve out the customers until they've gnawed
the last semi-defrosted fish finger
and devoured the smacked bottoms of raw battery chickens!

Then send in the delicacies,
tapas variadas de Sant Jordi Orwell:
mini stotties (Stotticitas! with smear of pease pud
topped with a sliver of boiled ham;
Craster kippers formed into stylish little shoes and handbags
in the Carrer de Crasteria;
Greased Puffin Breast in a Batter Burrow;
Tripe Smiles in Hangover Broth;
Gurnard Cheeks Trapped in a Basket (woven from
their own pink finger-fins)!

Homage to Picasso the Inquisitor of Rain

In the rainy actual *placa* de Jordi Orwell
around the chocolate table in *La Concha*
where all the colours muted out of its fawn fitting
are turned up on the little TV to their tangerine max
even as we're being cheated for squid & tortilla
I realise that this dark and shabby weather
is a dalek designed by Picasso, bringing us our bill
on a salver made of compacted salt and slavers.

The pigeons puff out feathers in the gaps
in the wall of Sant Maria del Mar, become
cubes of fluffy rat flesh; bagsnatchers leap prams
in the slick streets outside the Catedral
where the smell of rain mingles with incense
at the entrance to the cloisters. A girl kisses
the hand of the man holding an umbrella over her
and I go in: the Roman geese that fill the garden have
little tufts like candle flames on their warning heads.
Two men lower a stick over which
holy vestments have been stretchered
into a brazier and the flame shoots up, Pentecostal.

In *El Quatre Gats*, Picasso kicks me in the back
so I can hardly walk past the *Clansman* Bar
(see Celtic Six v. Partick Thistle Nil this Sunday) to his Museu,
where an origami Velasquez stuffing doves
into shoeboxes yolked with Provencal dawns
states 'I don't have an imagination
                                    I have an inquisition'.

I bow beneath the interrogation of the rain.

Vision and Prophecy of Newcastle Yet to Come

Here I see the ghost of my adopted city huddled and complete:
Newcastle, here is your amputated limb's *mesura*,
in this Gothic Quarter that still itches in
your galleries and on your tourist information boards.
You haunt these streets each possessed of one trade's memories:
sombreros, the toucan jaws of scissors,
pigskin stilettos, sharpeners and grainier paper,
chapel candles, cinnamon and roasted almonds:
here is what you've lost to qualify for modernity.

Here is why Akenside never smiled, writing on bacon rinds
among the sawdust shambles of his father's butcher shop.
Here is why Martin humped Sodom on Gomorrah
and burned them both in a clear chilli oil
(how desperate fun always sounds in the Bible
like the laughter of arthropods, bubbling in fishcrates),
Lot's wife like a salt cellar on the counter of a Grainger Market caff.

In the city yet to come there shall be eyes
in the palms of all the goalkeepers' seraphic hands.
There shall be a tiny spot of verdigris
on the Adam's apple of the Geordie bourgeoisie.
All bookmarks shall be blackened green peppers.
The rose shall be equal to the book,
in fact all books shall be assembled
in the shape of roses:
their perfume of old rotted librarian
shall be prized along the Rambla Saint James.

And in the heart of every rose there shall be a sick anchovy.

Homage to Jamon

I saw a pig's trotter sticking in Julia's ear
in the *Can Massano* restaurant
as though she was receiving messages
from Radio Free Trotter,
from irate carcasses,
and all coathooks and handles became
deep-fried curlicue aerials
of pigtails and pintles.

Didn't you always want to be
in telepathic contact with a pig?
Haven't you heard them transmitting from the pirate sty
how they were our irresistible substitute
for eating each other?
Don't even vegetarians snort and roll at night
in lucid *morcilla*-devouring visions?
Haven't you awoken from the cut-throat dream
knowing exactly what parts of everybody's flanks
you'd slice and cure and eat?

Tell me you'd not drink Circe's flask
of soya milk-based smoothie juice
laced with extracts from medieval parchments
from the *Ars Compendiosa Inveniendi Veritatem*
and let yourself become
an edible one?
A delible mark on the plates of Catalonia,
a delicacy who can describe its own consumption.

Think of the colour of your own serrated flesh:
the honey and beetroot varnished pane
you're sure they fitted into wattle hut frames
back when you'd slit your own throat at Michaelmas
and salt your quartered hanging flesh
and seal your house against the sleet
with drumskin meat, snow-fat cataracts
while you became your own hamfisted, stock-bone furniture.

Praise to the horizontal humans
who make lampshades from their own *jamon*
who make magic lanterns from their spinning hips
and crackling, on which they cast
the movie that we still can't watch
in which a well-stropped cloud is drawn across
the eyeball of Sylvia Plath.

Chorus of Skin and Screaming

> 'We see shoemakers take leather and stretch it and anoint it, to make it soft; and then we see them cut and sew it. And so, Lord, I see how your skin was stretched on the Cross, and bathed in blood, and torn and broken and pierced; and there was no man to heal and sew up your wounds.'
> Ramon Llull, *Llibre de Contemplacio de Deu*

When a boy fell into a vat of boiling dye
in his father's factory,
Claudio Guell, heir to the same fortune
that paid for the Palau, the Parc and the Crypt
where Gaudi plagiarised from 'the Great Book'
was ordered to provide a skin graft.

After this, twenty workers followed suit,
and finally Santiago, the second son.
For contributing their vellum to
this automatic *Llibre de Gremial dels Sabaters*
the boys received titles,
the employees were given plasters.

Homage to the Siesta of the Moustaches

'Donde hay pela hay alegria'

Here they come into the *Palau* of Dry Noise:
the facial hairs of Wilfred the Hairy,
moth-shaped founder of Catalunya; and those
of Mr Mustaches himself, *En Bigotos*, who
when he walks down the Carrer de Sant Pau
brushes the walls on either side
like a six foot woodlouse.

Hear the click of billiard balls beneath the *bigoti*,
the drooping moustache of the melancholic mayor;
the grinding together of six lumps of sugar within
the horizontal soufflé of the President of the *Diputacio*;
listen to domino tiles hit the marble tables
skewered on the royal antennae favoured by Dalí
who mutters in his sleep:

'Physiological effects are not values in themselves...'
– a point disputed by the *mosca*, the fly-sized tuft
beneath the lower lip of a nearby radical
as the coffee spoons ring like crystal in the cups
concealed within *la patilla*, the muttonchop sideburns
which make a former mayor's face look like
bacalla, a split and salted cod.

Hours slip by, and all one's headaches are bearable
if cradled by a moustache; compared to the airship on
your upper lip, compared to the smoke
of Carunchas, of Murias, of Havana,
all weaving themselves into deliciously perfumed
bluish and elegant air moustaches,
all is *seny*, all is solid.

What do moustaches dream about? Beards.
And in the beard built from the light at the end
of the corridor, the green and soft light
of the Ramblas, trembling under plane trees,
the moustaches locate their *Museu Sentimental*,
weaving into its edible nests
their rasping paeans to repetition.

Homage to Lampshades

Praise to the lampshades of Barcelona
warmed by tapas, hot throats and cigarettes
in the atrabilious air of restaurants
we'll never pass again, your marriages
between orchids and squid sacs,
your distended megaphones
with waterstains around the rims,
your discovery of the opposite of kidneys.

Orange ochre rows of you in *La Concha*,
low over the counter like autumnal ceps;
long cylindrical reedy lampshades
in the smeary pencil-case-shaped bar
next door, like bushels of sun;
upended baskets with dense mesh
in *Connibio*, inside each of you
a single vertical striplight glowering
like a slit window in a woven tower,
a straw helmet for a Catalan Cyclops.

Praise to you, inner nebulae, raybans of the lightbulb,
praise to you for shading our wobbling eyeballs from
those multiple, fly-murdering suns;
cheekguards that keep blinding Apollo in check,
contraceptives of light,
seroxat pillules that keep us all from seeing
exactly what is on the ends of all our forks,
praise to you, lampshades of the Anxious City!

Lament for the Improvements of Modernist Newcastle

It's the loss of these conglomerated pends, wynds and chares
burned in the idolatry of concrete
that makes Bewick's birds sing of *enyoranca*
and the angelic maggots wriggling from the palm
of T. Dan's hand
                join in this slogan-psalm:
'Not coal but call centres,
not mackerel but the Metro Centre,
not a centre but a brand name discount facility.'

Newcastle is 55° North of where everyone is staring
down the barrel of the Ramblas at the finger
of Christopher Rectal Examination Colon
vaguely pointing in the wrong direction for America
though every direction eventually reaches America
if, like Newcastle, you gradually shed all clothing and language
and float there clinging to inflated peanuts, hiding in footballs,
on rafts made of cotton buds with disposable nappy sails.

The twenty foot fibreglass *gambas* Mariscal put
on the seafront sings '*Caca i carbo*' (cack and coal)
and the Roma children beat it with sticks
till it shits football strips
                and so we know we are at home
in the phantom intestine of Newcastle
evacuating in the harbour at Barceloneta
all the desires and jaundices like rain
that Geordies store in the cheeks of their colossi,
the lighthouses of Shearer and Jackie Millburn
flanking our Toon as Barcelona is flanked by
                Tibidabo, Montjuic,
heads like rainclouds that can never burst.

Here in the drizzle and the shoeleak
all that grey Northern water is finally allowed to fall
in a *rauxa* of grief, in a mafficking, a B-day release.

Revenant

Too weak to more than tap upon the wrong-paint door
      there ought to be a key that he no longer has
a shuffling in in slippers now he cannot speak
      you are a stranger in the way that seems at home
the house as was now ends upon the kitchen step
      from there on in it isn't and the back wall's skull
has opened and the names for here stepped out or fell
      a scrabble for the number at the hospital
a cardigan for four miles and his nose runs cold
      and all the sheds where he developed shots are gone
a barn-big sitting room that guts those ghosts of brick
      there is another threshold here he cannot cross
those orange washes and the violet-smeared walls
      there is a corner where the sink would like to be
the spatters of his arteries are now white matt
      he lies on varnished timber and the vanished rug
the sense of an old woman you appeased with flowers
      the nurses had to jump into a colleague's car
asperging all the bedrooms, wooden sword in hand
      he can no longer tell you how he curls there, safe
a cushion underneath his head, your own old blanket
      the nurses can't imagine how he got this far
how he regarded something through you in the walls
      the thing that you can still call home surviving much
the sense of how to get there what you don't yet know.

neareast

Afterwards

It seems that I've arrived here afterwards,
but Sofia, named for wisdom, doesn't say:
the world I've missed won't sit in any words.

It was the same in Moscow, Beijing – blurred
by jetlag, all the stars were rolled away
they told me, and I'd landed afterwards.

The statutes rip, the statues tip, the birds
return to sing upon dictators' graves –
the world's a mist that shifts, in other words.

So Palaeologos, lost in sickle swords,
threw Byzantium and his purple robe away,
then I arrived, long after afterwards.

And even in my own land, all the hoards
are long since ransacked and their skulls displayed,
the world I've missed won't fit in canny words.

So Sofia, swaddled in the empires' shrouds,
lets me discover her in disarray.
I know that I've arrived at afterwards,
and the world, once missed, must unseat all our words.

An Approach to Sofia

So much plaster has fallen from her walls
she feels like *lokum* or an unpeeled lychee
with its stalk still attached but not to a bush.
Down the side of an apartment block
in yellow visiting letters it says SOFCOM.

The light switches in the agency hostel are round
like discoloured eyeballs in black sockets.
Old gloss drips across the eyes of disenchanted
journalists. Flick them and they sound like big fat drops
on big fat roses; click, and the drops sound cold.

The Largo's yellow bricks taste of a dust
that you suspect is a worn-out turmeric.
The space where Zhivkov's tomb used to be
looks like the bristly disconnected jaw
of Desperate Dan, looks like a colossal chin.

Sitting on a stump with her black-clad back
to Vassil Levski Stadium, the art student sketches
a giant submachine gun upheld beyond
the closed booths and bare trees. The city smells
of rain as it is anticipated, rain as it falls.

Ghost Guests

The staff at the Bulgarian Telegraph Agency explain
our collaboration with the finest younger Bulgarian poets
must not disturb the ghosts of former journalists
who are still reporting events they can no longer attend,
that they never in fact attended,
who are typing up the news that never happened,
and quoting all the dignitaries
who still haven't spoken.

We must keep shtum: there are typewriters inside
those small dead skulls
still clacking dryly into the limestone
of keen journalistic frontal lobes,
and the ghosts, who do not sleep above us,
must not be distracted – even by our clicking
Esperanto *na billiardski* – especially while
the staff attempt to watch Juventus.

The staff's large dogs either protect us
from wolves, mafia, and owl-shaped assassins,
or they prevent us from leaving.
Like the ghosts, thirsty for unbroken stories,
they sprawl around all day
while we, guests of a genus
unable to shower or buy *Zagorka* beer,
advance the dialogue of nations.

Hram-Pametnik Aleksander Nevski

'Hope allows us to deceive ourselves into thinking that life is parcelled into discrete chunks – that our lives are stories with beginnings, middles and ends.'
                              David Byrne, *The New Sins*

This whole cathedral feels inverted by
its brightly white-walled, icon packed-out crypt;
that groaning well above more like a pit,
a funnel into earth instead of sky.

Post-Ottoman, it's only a reflection
of what these panels would have liked to found:
a nation's birth delivered through the wounds
that Georgi and Dimitar took with unction

and here inflict on dragon and on Turk
in mirrored blows, these warrior saints who poise
their name days at the seasons' gates, who pose
on rearing mounts against their dawns and darks

like scissors snipping out the fissive truth
that centuries can pass without a hope
while rebel songs meet silence on a rope –
this whole room's painted by those dying breaths.

It's in the miracle – that boy, unsure-
ly perched behind Georgi, somehow plucked
from the emir's side, still gripping at the jug
of Cretan water he was poised to pour.

It's in the ready martyrdoms – these rows
of butchered haloes who all trust their fears
will writhe upon Dimitar's needle spear –
he shakes his beard and it begins to snow.

And later at the launch for some new book
that claims to know our sins' new names, folk yelled
and drank wine like a hive of infidels,
till in the middle of that mell I looked

across to the cathedral through a square
of statues sinking into snow, as though
we'd drunk or cursed above into below,
and made earth cloud, and all these crystals prayers.

I went out, felt the chill and watched the flakes
ascend to line the statues' lids with grief
or paint flecks, those white letters that belief
forms from the gasps we force from dying necks.

Dvoyanka

Last night we ate from *Unter den Linden*,
the Restaurant of the Knowledge of Enlightenment Europe
and Bulgarian Cuisine, and in between
the scything of the *gadulka* and laconic taps on a *tupan*,

I heard the double flute, that open-legged compass
of ancient, vase-based bacchanals – but chastened,
swung shut here, resembling a pencil case,
a long wood box emitting parallel melodies.

Later, we walked home past the vacant stone face
of a statue of former Socialist plenty,
clutching cold sheaves like corrected testaments,

and the *Sunshine Store*, selling stockings to a darkened street
upended limbs spidered with tights,
legs splayed in still colder display.

Red Lullaby

for Andy Croft

Hush little baby, don't feel worse,
Momma's going to buy you a talking horse,
a talking horse that wants to fly
and never tells a single lie.
The horse's mane is blow-torch white
to keep your crib aflame by night,
the horse's saddle strawberry red
to match the eyelids on your head,
the horse's hooves are made of steel
to keep your bedroom cold and real.
And if this truthful horse won't fly,
we'll bake its guts in humble pie;
and if this talking beast won't speak,
we'll dine on steak for half a week.

A Double Blessing

The mind makes bad museums out of time
in which it stacks the icons of the eye:
one hand, out of the host of hands they raised
to bless me – all Sofia's swarm of saints –
one hand distracts because beneath it floats
the sketch of its first gesture like a ghost.

Those fingers reach out for a different chord –
some *mudra* that just might have, like a sword,
split church from church, was painted over here
but not quite painted out. As sailors read
dawn air for traces of familiar islands,
I read a clutch of memories in that hand.

As children on our first small trips abroad,
its suns broke up our northern clouds like bread
and spread out foreignness as something sweet;
our palates knew already, as they ate
their strange new words that tasted old as earth,
arrival was a paradox like birth.

Small voyages – across the gilt lagoon
to Venice, built on pillaged holy loot,
or Varna's Roman boatyards, drowned out by
a giant statue for a giant lie,
that workers wanted what the Party willed:
I saw and didn't see what these concealed.

Till Kerkira rewrote an islet as
a ship caught up by metamorphosis:
just as its rudder rooted into rock,
that visual echo grounded myth in shock
and made Ulysses' exile seem as real,
as tactile as his petrifying keel.

The adult tightens his pedantic grip
upon the senses' helm: for him that ship
is overwhelmed by ideology;
each trip asserts its iconology
from failings and the failure to feel blessed,
departure seems another little death.

As mast and sail were blown to conifers,
a crew made owls or mice at some god's curse,
so every sainted hand and golden chapel
saw Venice reascribe Constantinople,
and that colossal isolated girl
called *wisdom* by a Socialistic world.

So fingers under fingers point us back
to what we hold and what our holdings lack:
inside Cyrillic sits its kin's physique,
long-boned Byzantium, that way that Greek
still spills that infants' glimpse of alphabet,
those hot geometries that hold our breath.

And so this doubled hand is like a film,
two cells imposed within a single frame
that show a cog of history begin
to turn: the present's never just a brim
beneath which an unreaching grip extends,
it is the blessing that we cannot end.

Portrait of an Informationist
(or, The Kind of Found Poetry I Want)

He dines only – or so he claims – on food that is pale:
eggs, sugar, shredded bones, the fat of dead animals.
His interests include: rare sea creatures, impossible machines,
forgotten local history, and the occult. He looks
like a startled owl, his hair swept back from
a glaring forehead, tufts around his ears, and eyes
wide open behind his pince-nez. He is evidently still drunk.
'We didn't eat every day, but we never missed an aperitif.
I remember a particular pair of trousers and a pair of shoes
that used to pass from one Informationist to the other,
and which we had to mend every morning.'

He plays knucklebones on the island. There is
a circle of standing skeletons in the middle distance.
He crushes the bones and puts the powder in an incense burner.
The smoke turns into cherub's wings, which flutter.
He collapses. The air turns white. A beautiful woman appears:
'It is the Church of Scotland!' She throws aside her cloak
and stands there in a gold tunic, looking like Wendy Wood.
He throws stones at her which turn into furballs.
There's a clap of thunder and the statues grind their teeth.
A volcano rises up in the middle of the island and spits stars.
When he comes to, he has a beard, and his hair has turned white.
She keeps two cats to whom she feeds herring on Fridays
which she describes as 'good Catholics', as well as a goat
in Rangers shorts, who eats any verse which doesn't please her.

He comes into some money in 1997, and immediately blows it
on seven identical chestnut-coloured corduroy kilts,
acquiring the nickname 'Velvet Donkey' from his fellow poets.
Every day he walks the 55 miles from Drem to Croy,
setting off in the morning with his umbrella tucked under his arm,
and staggering back in the small hours. He claims
never to have taken the bus. He carries a hammer
for protection as he crosses the bandit-ridden stretch
between Dechmont and Torphichen.
When talking he will stop, bend one knee a little,
adjust his pince-nez, and place his fist on his hip.

'"Facts about Sea Cucumbers" is the first of the suite
Scotland is Another Country Underneath the Sea,
which begins by explaining what eating a sea cucumber is like.'
It apparently resembles chewing a tenderised eraser.
'Ignorant people call them "hollow thuribles".' Later,
he describes the sea cucumber as 'purring like a nightingale
with toothache'. The ninth part, 'Golf and the Cuttlefish',
describes a cuttlefish's comeuppance on the sunken links:
'The cuttlefish's skin is a shocking tweedy green.
He chirrups he will be victorious. His caddie,
a haddie, follows him, carrying his clubs.
The lobsters are amazed.
The holes are all a-tremble: the cuttlefish is here!
And now he is playing his shot:
His muscular hydrostat flies into pieces!'
His last words are 'Ah! The coos...' Then
he takes off once more with small, deliberate steps.

It seems impossible that he lives in such poverty.
The man has literally nothing worth a shilling:
a wretched bed; a table covered with forks and knives
and walking sticks of various sizes,
all clattering together in despair; one chair;
and a half-empty wardrobe in which there are
a dozen old-fashioned corduroy kilts,
never worn and almost identical.
In each corner of the room
are piles of old newspapers and old hats, softening
the noises of the cutlery, the clubs, and the sticks.

Note: this poem draws in its entirety on an article by Nick Richardson on Satie. See 'Velvet Gentleman' (LRB, 4 June 2015)

**Murder
Bear**

The Four Bears

Of course Daddy Bear never mentioned
his missing brother, Murder, nor that
he wasn't missing at all, but in the loft
the whole time Baby Bear was downstairs
in the bed beside Mummy's and Daddy's
dreaming about a girl who once lay between
his sheets, who perfumes his pillow still
with her grassy fresh air sweat. Had we all
been aware that it was Murder Bear
who fell down the ladder like a shadow,
crossing out the sunlight cast through
the curtain in the shower, and took off
a cloud of her golden hair with one claw
and most of her face with the other,
we should not have been so anxious
to lock Baby Bear's mother and father up
in Polar Penitentiary. How Daddy Bear
persuaded the others not to squeal
we do not know. Only that after the trial
Baby returned to the disembowelled house
(his uncle having fled into the forest
to dwell among the gory leavings of Autumn),
there to sleep in the same bed, eat
at the same table, and contemplate
the temperature of the blood that pours
through his veins. It's Baby Bear temperature.
Upon the plain scrubbed table before him
remains her bowl, filled with golden hair.

A Night Story

Once upon a time there was a Murder Bear.
Then he killed everyone. The End.

...Why aren't you asleep yet?
'You frightened me talking about Murder Bear.'

Well, you don't need to be afraid of Murder Bear unless he finds you.
'He isn't going to find me, is he?'

Yes. Yes he is going to find you:
Murder Bear finds everyone eventually.

'How can he tell?'
By your sweet, sweet smell.

'Does he kill everyone?'
D'uh. The clue is in the name.

'Does he kill Goldilocks?'
'Goldilocks is no longer with us.'

'Does he kill Paddington?'
Yes, he really goes to town on Paddington.

'Does he kill Postman Pat?'
He beats him to death with his own cat.

'Does he kill Blue Peter?'
With a parking meter.

'Does he kill News at Ten?'
With a fountain pen.

'Does he kill the X Factor?'
He takes the judges out with a tractor.

'Does he kill Harry Potter?'
There is a considerable amount of JK Rowling-related slaughter.

'When is he coming for me?'
Once he's dealt with your poor parental units.

'You can beat him, though, can't you?'
I thought I'd explained there really is no hope. Now go to sleep.

...'Night night.'
Night, Honey Bun.

Murder Bear and the Makie-Up People

Murder Bear kept his honey in a row
of skulls along the mantelpiece although
these were the noggins of fictional detectives.
But as he'd neither fire nor place to rest
his wiry head, that hardly seemed to matter.
Mater Ursus used to leave him notes concerning
the whereabouts of bootprints of the novelists:
'By the trail of paper entrails ye shall know them...'
'...and by the ten thousand flapping ghosts
of golden luckless lasses I shall hunt them down,
for Jesus saith...' he'd reply, not at all averse
to the removal of scripture from its abdomen
by keyhole claw, 'that 'Whosoever looketh on
the genre of horribly-tortured women
hath committed Murder Bear unto his heart'.
'And anyway...' – bursting through the chalet walls
in a conversational tone, walls that once had looked
so stout of timber and now were found to be
a forgery in Toblerone and matchwood –
'you have to excorticate to desanguinate,
or, othergates, butcher the scribblers before
they can kill off their darkling constables
and other dicks...'; ripping out their sinful hearts
and shameful tongues, and bearing back
their thumbs and delicious typing appendages
to roast upon his flameless forest grate.

A Murderous Sestina

'You don't really come here for the hunting, do you?'

Murder Bear knows nothing of humour, only the thunder
between his temples that announces another apartment
must be varnished in blood before the flit up country
to where mist makes the mountains frown. But pleasant
ribaldry dictates that in these woods, buttocks scratched
with Twig Sumerian, teeth flecked with spinach,

a hunter must cower behind – what is this, spinach?
How would he know? – while the roar like thunder
of a grizzly, enraged at his bullet that has scratched
her shoulder, reverberates within the log apartment
he'd rented for the weekend, thinking it would be pleasant
to reconnect with someone's roots, far from Rutabaga County,

which is why Murder Bear briefly considers country
matters, given the joke's logic and the quantities of spinach
he's eaten en route, lending a not-unpleasant
vigour to his step and other appetites, but thunder
announces our autumnal rains, so to the apartment
he repairs, its furniture much chewed and scratched

by the grizzly, a dear coz whose head he'd scritched
when she was GRARGH-high back in that other country
before the first neck-snappings. They tidy the apartment
and have dinner – venison steaks and further spinach;
while the hunter times his howls to match the thunder
they spend a firelit hour in complicit pleasantries,

as though Cape Fear could ever be Mount Pleasant,
but soon blind rage returns, the way that lightning has scratched
out the hunter's eyes – a need inevitable as thunder
drives MB twitch-clawed out into night's country
to shred his victim's skin as though a chard or spinach,
then burn him shrieking in his well-insured apartment.

Next morning, kicking through the spars of the apartment,
he finds the hunter's trousers, folded and complacent
upon a blackened chair, remembers the spinach
between those knocked-out teeth, and sees he's barely scratched
the surface of his cousin or this fucked-up country,
feeling as stupid as the lisping God of Thunder,

Thor. There's still tinned spinach in the apartment –
she's gone like lightning, but, thunderously humming pleasant
airs, he follows her message north, scratched across his country.

from Murder Bear's Address to the Polar Explorers

...I see you're not as fascinated by the way
the page makes so strange a mirror
to our imagined meanings as am I.
Your eyes are far more drawn to this
ice-axe: perhaps you wonder how,
thumb-less, I grip it so very tightly.
And yet you came here to ask
a similar question of all this snow:

'What can we mean where we do not matter?'
and not, 'Who is the Bear that stalks beside you?'

If you were indeed taught writing by a bird
(Thoth, that long-legged god of the papyrus);
then warned against it by a wise Athenian
(Socrates, fearing the murder of memory);
next, advised *contre interpretation* by
of all nationalities a Frenchman
(my dear Montaigne, who schools you
not to 'fill posterity with crotchets'),

then where shall paradox end but on the edge
of this, your finely-honed ice-axe?
It is the space in the beast which concerns you
here, to reverse language's polarity –
that which does not come across
to you, cranial astronauts, who cannot know
how I do not think I am and therefore must
travel to your inner stars' menageries,
dig to your circus of the lower rings: limbic,
reptile, then the notochordate worm.

See how the ice-axe gleams in the brevity
of the sun: think of it as Hackem's Razor.
I shall address you and these questions to
the crevasse, since it never asks
and cannot answer the blue telephone
far below, like a meaning in an ink-stroke
pressed into this page of flattened stars
like an anti-mountain, mould for Mont Blanc –
its call is valuable to us: please pick up
if it should ring while you are passing.

The Passionate Psychobear to His Love

Come dine with me and share this rug
and shrive our guilt with half a shrug:
the lovers who dined here before
won't need their picnic anymore.

They've set aside first fork and glass
then mortal things – all this must pass;
and should their heads prove hard to find
their fingers still lie here entwined.

That salmon slapping on your plate:
bite off its tail – it shan't escape;
then with my littlest claw...now, lo!
observe its pomegranate roe.

Each rosy orb that parts your lips
shall add unto the blood eclipse
I'll visit on the fauna which
disturb our realm with fence and ditch.

Each logger, jogger, fisher, witch
shall find their hike has met its hitch:
I'll raise you a mountain from their arms,
though off they run with shrill alarums.

This wilderness shall be your park:
no nightingale disturbs your dark –
the shriek-owl's song's more to our taste.
All this for you I shall lay waste.

All seasons must bow down before
your gelid eye, or drown in gore:
this bucket for your throne of ice,
gaze on our ursine paradise.

Bear Grills Bear Grylls

Survivo-journalistics rarely outlived a day
    in the company of Murder Bear –
ephemerons and mumble-newses to his purview,
    they learnt to rue that urge to interview
which drove them to his hills, rich in pineals,
    where he'd scoop their quaking innards
onto the barbecue. Hanging with him was not
    drawn-out in such close quarters
where he'd query, 'Learn to share: what was it
    in your upbringing led you to suppose
everyone could be reduced to a mere *mots jus*?'
    Woodsmen didn't take to his tendency
to reuse their signature sinews and living ligaments
    as catapults, sending evidences of
our frail humanities through the forest canopies
    to be picked over by editor jays,
scat-speckled squirrels and bespectacled pies.
    Smears of Ray Mears still appear,
contaminating crime labs and delis across
    three states. Though Butcher Bird
and Carrion Crow study the DVD evidence
    of his interrogation technique,
all he'll say of The Death of a Thousand Offcuts is
    'The victim needs no expertise.'

Hellbeareen

Murder Bear liked to disguise himself as the ghost
of a small boy when it was time to walk among
the spirits and enquire which did homeowners prefer,
tragedy or terror? They would lean down to correct him,
'I think you'll find it's trick or...' – only to see ichor
start to pour from the child's eyes and nose and ears,
and hear behind them the scorching hiss of tar
slumping its way down their stairwell like a tongue,
unscrolling itself in pops and flickers, squeezing
between the banisters like mud through smoking teeth
and curling around their melting slippers – '...terror!'
the now-decayed urchin would conclude, before
reforming and heading next door. He loved our games,
and would often slip a drowned kitten or two
into the basin where the children dooked for apples,
or thread a libertarian's liver onto the string
of treacle-dunked scones. Nothing delighted him more
than substituting for a pumpkin the flaming head
of a much-loved teacher, or intricately carving a neep
into an anatomically correct inverted platypus.
Come midnight he would lead a dancing host
of rot-shrouded skullheads through town as
the sky filled with ghost riders trailing horse guts,
and daub the splintering doors of cowering householders
with a paw replenished by dips in a boiling tureen
of blood and borscht, borne on the back of the skeleton
of a giant turtle raised by his necromantic skills,
while bellowing theatrically, 'Bring out your living!'

Hendecakillabics for the Restive Season

In the month of the marked increase in shopping
by his donning a slightly-chewed-up man-suit
(victim chosen for having such a fat head,
though it's still quite a squeeze to cram his ears in),
the most murderous of bears will pass among us
on the metro, the bus, the escalator,
in the cafes and bars that warm large cities,
and select his exciting Christmas victim.
While old humbugs may sit unscathed beside him,
the unduly punctilious buyers of slippers
and insisters on proper thankyou letters
may expect an unusual midnight visit
and their neatly-wrapped skin ripped open roughly
till their seasonal lights festoon the fir tree.
'Tis the time of the year to clean his rifle
as he hopes that old fool presents a target
he can aim at upon the yuletide rooftops,
then it's out with the hunting knife for Rudolf.
In the meantime there's always office parties
to be crashed and then photocopied bleeding
from each orifice; boss and secretary
bound together and flung into the river
in a touching noyade of class relations.
Always drunks to be nudged off station platforms,
little match-girls to sautee by flame-thrower,
snowmen needing to eat their magic top-hats,
anxious mothers who must see all their trimmings,
lazy fathers who need a shot of buckshot.
It's a miracle how he gets around us
all in just one night, but a bear must do in
whom a bear (so the voices claim) must do in.
So you be just as good, or bad, or ugly
as your conscience sees fit, because the main thing's

to be lucky and quick and unobtrusive
like a rat or a strain of flu or music
that might soothe this most savage beast: no carols,
please, unless you can live without your larynx,
though a phrase from the Stranglers or old Sweeney
(if your whistle be wet) might mean he walks on
by, the wing of Death's angel fails to beat in
your face, eyes screwed shut, heart, for now, still beating;
heart still serving up blood in pints. Go, bootsteps;
heart, relax; and those nails, release the brickwork –
then his whisper: '*I hear you when you're weeping...*'

Didst Thou Ever See Murder Bear?

a Shandean Digression & Found Poem

MURDER BEAR! Very well.
Have I ever seen him?
Might I ever have seen him?
Am I ever to see him?
Ought I ever to see him?
Or can I ever see him?

Would I had seen Murder Bear!
(for how can I imagine it?)
If I should see Murder Bear,
what should I say?
If I should never see Murder Bear,
what then?

If I never have, can, must or shall
see Murder Bear alive;
have I ever seen him dead?
If so, which of us was thus?
Did I ever see him painted? – described?
Have I ever dreamed of him?

Did my father, mother, brothers or sisters,
ever see Murder Bear?
What would they give?
How would they behave?
How would Murder Bear have behaved?
Is he wild? Tame? Terrible? Rough? Smooth?

– Is Murder Bear worth seeing? –
– Is there no sin in him? –
– Is he better than a TEDDY BEAR?

Murder Bear Has the Last Words

Murder Bear was an endgame hunter, and indeed,
as the Amazon River Dolphin found out, fisher.
Once he'd played midnight's chimes to the Sun Bear,
and was Cassandra to the ultimate Panda;

once he'd been an Ahab to the Gobi Bear
('How a harpoon in the desert amazes the Mazaalai!')
and had made a spectacle of Tremarctos Ornatus
('A giant burning lens focuses both mind and eye!),

he turned to the terminal languages, sitting
with their grey-faced speakers for hours, grizzling
along, mastering the lilt if not the meaning,
as they told their fables for the final time.

When he heard the two last speakers of Ayapeneco
refused to talk to each other, he determined
to referee between them, as to who should truly
have the last word, which only he would hear.

Some tongues he collected like stamps –
Gaelic and Aramaic fascinated:
their dialects of Cain and Judas spoke to him;
he mouthed the phrasebooks of murder and betrayal.

He dealt with the alphabets alphabetically
murmuring, 'Ainu, Bo, Cayuga, Dumi,
Evenki, Faroese, Guajiro...'. With the ideographs
he hit upon the graphic art of kill-igraphy.

He heard them plead their hopeless cases,
then laid out their dead declensions, mourning
as their dictionaries burned, 'I like a corpse
in cuneiform'; and keening, 'Ate in Akkadia, Urso.'

He sought, in those broken-off last words
a different eloquence, and set about him
to reduce the world to its original dumbness,
a garden filled with that silence before sin

could be spoken of...

Murdered Sonnet

A reification a taxonomy and a teleology
walked into the bar where Murder Bear was in mid-
Stagger mode with a handgun and a hopelessness –
murderer of childhood's dream that every fate
is random but for yours, each death inevitable
except I shall be spared; killer of the ease
with which we believe that narrative applies
to our dreams and not to how we remember them;

despoiler of the garden where the wrinkles are
just tiredness, the hair loss only stress, and, look!
picker-offer of the dead as they return to us
over the river and under the trees, just as
they always said they would in the movie
where the hero is being eaten by his friend the bear.

Montaigne and the Three Murder Bears

Rain-allowing Graskolnikov asks Moosebuggery
who is this third whom the weather detains,
who glares fit to kill since we are too merry,
awaiting the approach of Monsieur de Montaigne?

Who is this third whom the weather detains,
who fidgets through packages under the trees,
awaiting the approach of Monsieur de Montaigne?
Perhaps he is counting his murderer's fee?

He who fidgets through packages under the trees
may well prove too nervous when in at the kill.
Perhaps he is doubting this murderous spree?
But no, he's located a box full of pills.

Those who get nervous when in at the kill
take physic from sack, read fortune from signs,
or else take their courage from boxes of pills –
but no, he has drawn and is first in the line.

Take physic from sack and read fortune from signs
your death is upon you, Monsieur de Montaigne!
But no, though he's drawn and is first in the line,
he's gifting him pills and not giving him pains...

'When death is upon you, Monsieur de Montaigne,'
he whispers, while swinging his cutlass at us,
'these pills for the quinsy and these for the pain.'
And now he has drawn a strange arquebus,

and whispers, while sweeping that weapon at us,
'Rain-hallowed Graskolnikov, Moosebuggery,
pray let your man go, says this primed arquebus,
or I will kill you both and then make most merry...'

Ours Meurtrière dans le Métro

'Here are men's memories and the ruins of their beliefs.'
Jean Cocteau

1
When Murder Bear dons his roller-skates
and descends by the Gare du Rue Morgue
into the necrotic *Métro*, he is always struck
by the apparition of thousands of *les jeunes
assassins femmes*, like lily leaves on the barrels
of Lugers, going about their girlish business
in *l'Enfers Gallique*. Here after all was where
he learnt Bearshido: the way of the wet work.
He puts on his raincoat, *son Samouraï feutre*.
'Ca va, Grand Ours,' says the head of Lambert
seconds after its decapitation by light saber.
'There can be only none,' MB replies, back-
heeling it into a crocheted basket.

2
He boards the phantom carriage which follows
every train, the one known as *Le Chat Mort
qui Rebondit* or *Le Coursier Funèbre*,
and hits the button which sends everything
à rebours. Gliding through the compartments,
he applies the brand 'Ça Plane' to Plastic Bertrand;
shoves Lacan back through the black mirror glass
with a single marigold; and pulls the chain
which starts the corkscrews in Proust's couchette.
To Mitterand he mutters, 'Je suis Charlotte,'
showering Nazi zombie ortolans into his hip-bath.
As the train flies through Abbesses he shouts
at the commuters, 'Là-bas the abyss!'

3
In *Le Dining Car* Baudelaire takes a toke and dons
his cheap toque, ready to hammer a duck flat
for his signature dish, *Les Fleurs du Mallard*.
Behind him Foucault flips eyeballs in a pan.
'These slices of Marcuse are still too thick,'
scolds the Bear. Below the place on the Place
de la Revolution where *Le Moulin à Silence* stood
he recites the code du jour into a lobster:
'In the month of Thermidor there will be boilings.
Trois fois.' The train divides like the legs
of a Can-Can dancer, and his half, shedding
screaming parts of passengers and their shredding
feuilletons, enters the catacomb of the animals.

4
Here the skulls are stacked by species –
an ossuary of the ox, a caprid crypt,
the bonehouse for canines – it is unclear who
or what burrowed out these corridors, lit
by luminescent tooth and horn, but
narcolepts placed in the necropolis report,
on waking and walking *les pavés*
of the dead streets to St Lazare (where an exit
has been provided) of shuffling processions:
human corpses with the fleshless heads
of beasts, chimeras dragging skeleton carts,
the elongating shadows and eroding echoes
of knuckle-rimmed wheels.

5
Murder Bear would like to meet one such
sad cavalcade, would like to think
he'd know them by their torsos alone
or their chewed and mangled feet.
He alights from the remains of the train.
Hefting his poleaxe, he shouts into
the fictive gloom, 'Neither come nor go
if you think you're Baudrillard enough!'
Never the leastest stir in the rust. 'Sous
la nouvelle vague, the latest plague!'
Around him and farther down the tunnels
the uncalled calls of the creatures swirl
like breath from the nostrils of a bull.

Dear Reader

Murder Bear shaved off all his bloody fur
and sat in the darkness of your kitchen
at the bare careful table you spent so long
scrubbing with salt, rubbing his pate like Kurtz.
The orange oblong of stairlight crayoned
by the doorframe made him grind his teeth.
He filled half the tumbler with Teachers
and topped it up with water. That would learn it.
He spread his papers across your table
and consulted the diagrams that stated
whether you would live or die. Because
he cannot hold the brush, he got you
to make these, although you never knew:
tore the letters from your lists, the glyphs
from your children's paintings, the ones
you'd filed away for later or forever,
you weren't sure, but – once he'd aligned them
according to those soft dictators, the moths,
discovered ideograms only the stars
should read, and let your kittens lick his claws –
he knew. You never saw a bear so alone.

Zeichentrickbärendämmerung

1

Only Booboo escaped to tell the tale
of the cartoon bears' big surprise picnic –
the postcard simply claimed, 'THE BLAME
IS YOURS ALONE'. Of course they knew
who it must be from: Murder Bear
has never been in the *Good Bear Guide*.
He punishes the good for when they're bad
and the vice-torn for versa: he is
an equal opportunities ursa; also an
omnidirectional puncher of your sacred snouts;
pincher of the universal vagus; pitcher
of shrieking respectability into the tarpits;
he picks up any wasted rice grains
with other people's still-blinking eyelashes.
Plus the dank vermillion pawprint stank
of Parma Violets and horse entrails.
What to do? Well, if there's a murder in Mordor
who you gonna call – Orc-busters?
They kitted up with harpoons, hopelessness
and tasers; they googled for marmalade,
Mamelukes and razors; they goggled up with infra-red,
baked bread and broke out the Brens;
had a brew and filled flasks with liquid nitrogen
to fling in his face of monstrous doubt;
picked out the jams and the gelignite,
said goodnight ladies and sweet princes all
and convoyed by landcruiser for Jellystone...

2 Bonfire of the Teddy Bears

...where each morning Murder Bear would sit
at the feet of Yogi, although these
and his spiritual master's other bits
had to be kept in the deep freeze
overnight. 'What's that, Guru of gore?
deep in the woods prepare a pickernick
of slaying? Splatter there the average bear?
Get Rupert with a maverick spear?'
Baseball struck by Shoeless never soared so well,
so thunderous a Who-chord never burst
from Marshall stack. Like a crashing satellite
the war-lance (this he claimed to be the digit
of the Cherokee ogress, Spearfinger)
pierced the scarlet jumper's lower hem,
passed unchecked between his trousers' check
and, hissing, sank into the centre of his thigh.
He dumped po' Winnie's body in the well
and his head went bump, bump, bump
down after it, pondering in the last blink
of decapitated thought the distinction
between artesian and arterial, and
do bears eat chairs, or do chairs...
He then did aggro to Hair Bear's afro,
shaving a highway in that wilderness:
a road for the mind control electrodes
which meant, weeping, Aitch took care
of the Bunch himself, rubbed Bubbi up
the wrong way on the tongue-grater,
served Square rare as Forlorne Sausage...

3 *An Etiology of Murder Bear*

Who was not to be spared especially?
Baloo and Beorn to be shown the bare
excessities; Paddington and Shardik
to be shredded into bell jars; Sooty
to have the insanity claws inserted,
Biffo to drink invisible ink; the Hofmeister,
G, plus Fozzie, B, to sup with horrors, H;
from an island in Baffled Bay would-be
whale-watchers to hear a beluga's strangled cry,
'The Great God Alan Measles is dead!'

Thence to repair to a bar on 39th
between the river delta features of Wystan
and the large crow stabbing a shot glass,
and to bewail 'Gone, all gone; dead for
a duck-caller or possibly a duck-walk –
I got confused toward the end or even
the beginning – now how shall we ever know
the reason why, O rare Mongolian Bear,
or Spirit Bear of British Columbia, or...' (a pause)
'insert a third bear species of your choosing...'

That giant faithless head, that would crush
a shoulder, crashing to the bar; a snore,
that rattled Dylan in St James Infirmary
as though he were a bottle on a shelf;
while across the nation, in a daze,
husbands put down axes, wives
relinquish knives, punks step away from
the pistol; sickles, pitchforks, lose their gleam,
professors pause at chalkboards, poets
put down their glasses and their pens.

Goldilocks comes out of the shower and says
to the dilating eyes of Baby Bear:
'What a strange dream I had, Babes.'
I know, Honey, I know: I was there.

*

Exeunt omnes, pursued by Murder Bear

Little Instruments of Apprehension

the wreckage that floats on the eyeball
an earhole's slimy bung
the noisome air in the nostrils
a metal taste on the tongue
the feel of fire in the fingers' tips:
with these the world's begun

(goggles & eyedrops)

*vliegbrillen/occhiali/anteojos protectors
støvbriller/snøbriller/syze dielli ë
lunettes/Schutzbrille/tarashit glaza
portholes for the eyeship/gia ta matia*

*pika për syrin/customised rain
gouttes pour les yeux/Augentropfen
stagones/gia ta matia/di1 yan3 ye4
colirio/oogdruppels/prodigal tears*

King Heart lives in his bony house
all walled about by skin
counting all the ways the world
can send invaders in

*Waterglass and needle, contact lens and cut
earhole and eyeball, gullet gob and gut*

There's sluice ports in his sea walls and
he's shiteholes on the land
where fate sees opportunity
to undermine command

Waterglass and needle, contact lens and cut
earhole and eyeball, gullet gob and gut

There's swine fly past his turrets while
he swears he's still too young
to meet his Maker's viruses
that make us speak in tongues

(earmuffs, earplugs & cotton buds)

fur headphones/nowshniki/casques anti bruit
veshore/orejeras/Gehörschutz
oorberschermers/øreklapper/paraorecchie
Princess Leia skull doughnuts/gia ta aftia

tappo per le occhie/er3 sai1/øreprop
boule Quies/øreplugger/burrowers in wax
oordopjes/tapa veshësh/otoaspides
translators of the sirens into distance

bomullsknopper/ørepinde
wattenstaafjes/coton-tiges
bastoncillo de algodon/gonxhe pambuku
dumbbells for mice/xilakia

Choruses of locusts bring
a plague into his houses
Miasmas fill the shopping mall
with mozzies mites and louses

Doorhandle worktop toilet seat and towel
nasal passage windpipe ear canal and bowel

The bugs hear everything he prays
the rats sink all his shipping
his drains are ripe with crocodiles
his veins are lined with dripping

Doorhandle worktop toilet seat and towel
nasal passage windpipe ear canal and bowel

such tiny cudgels he must wield
such micro-spears and armour
he's nothing small enough to shield
the body's open harbours

(noseclips & facemasks)

klip mitis/neusknijpers
naeseklemmer/strong
morsetto/pince-odeurs
kapëse hundësh/pong

mascarilla/masque/chirurgical
Gesichtsmaske/maska prosopou
maschera facciale/ansigtsmasker
mian4 zhao4/sail of the nose mast

'Five servitors this king he had without
That teachit were aye treason to espy;
They watchit aye the walls round about
For enemies that of happening come by.'

(toothpicks & gags)

tandstikker/palillo/stuzzicadenti
tandenstoker/odontoglyphida/mondadientes
tandpetare/palito/chachalitsa
tannpirker/Zahnstocher/cure-dents

zatichka/mordaza/a blindfold for the gob
mundkurve/baillon/Knebel/prop
tapa/a sellotape for speak
fimotro/bavaglio/stop

Though water loves bacteria
and air still cradles ills
we must excrete hysteria
the world is not a pill

Sunlight and wineglass pillowbook and song
pleasure is the weakness that makes us strong

We all shall eat a peck of dirt
and drink a pint of piss
clean our teeth on dirty shirts
but life is more than this

Sunlight and wineglass pillowbook and song
pleasure is the weakness that makes us strong

Let basilisks of bacillae
turn everything to stone
we still must open mouth and eye
and face the sun alone

(nailclippers, gauntlets & surgical gloves)

Nagelknipser/cortaunyas
nyhokoptis/coup-ongles/darë
Nagelschaaren/tronchesina
neglesaks/zhi3 jia3 dao1

Panzerhandschuhe/nettle-graspwear
kravehandsker/gant/dorashka
latnaya rukaveetsa /bitten mitten/don't
touch/la manopla/di blah di/gant

guanti medicali in lattice/latekshansker
Gummihandschuhe/ru3 jiao1 shou3 tao4
skin of the five-limbed examiner
gadia apo latex/doreza sanitare

a fresh lake's brim on the eyeball
the ear, all music's home
a halesome breath in the nostrils
the salt tang on the tongue
a feel of silk in the fingers' tips:
with these our day is done.

Don Juan's Pilgrimage

'...I must be fated
To wander and to change; when the mast creaks
I smell the salt and know my soul unsated
Until it finds the language no man speaks.'
Edwin Morgan

'Thus the doors of the sea and the keys
of the universe, with anything of a reasonable
sort of management, will of course enable its
proprietors to give laws to both oceans...'
William Paterson

'Look at the map.'
Chekhov

'J'ai seul la clef de cette parade sauvage.'
Rimbaud

1
I met him in Caracas on the Mount,
a sermoniser from the outset, one
who shouts in mirrors, loud as life: the Count,
slumped in a darkened cable car, alone,
apart from that quick voice; Milord, that fount
of filth and fiery judgement – anglophone
but with Hispanic hints, all lisp and spit
dangling above the forest's tropic pit.

2
He had, he told me, taken on a floor
of that disused hotel, the Humboldt, high
cylinder, symbol of the wealth before
Chavez, before all Castro's hopeful lies,
Peron's romance of truth. Paused at the door,
he apologised before I'd half-surmised
his motive, strode to open curtains on
fit Caribbean backdrop to – the Don.

3
Over a cheap *arepa* at the State-
sponsored cafe, he told me how he'd bribed
a pretty tour guide for the key – he'd hate
to get her into trouble, but described
his *Callipygita* so intimate-
ly that the sort of trouble was transcribed
into a tender cursive by his mouth –
I asked how long had he adored the South?

4
'I came here on a Dundee merchant ship
as junior engineer. I crawled its keel,
the long propeller shaft, and felt the grip
of tides along its vertebrae of steel.
We docked at Demerara's sugared hips,
and drank until the Scotsmen couldn't reel.
I challenged one to swim the brown-lipped river –
they rescued me, but he went down to clabber.

5
'I jumped ship then and walked into the jungle,
took work on cane plantations, hopped planes north.
I hunted capybara, learned to mingle
with *Llanos* cowboys, *Guajiros* from the Firth
of Orinoco; played harp, got entangled
with Maracaibo oilmen's daughters worth
more than my life, so, jinking *mal' fortuna*,
sought haven on the islands of the Kuna...'

6
'Before you tell me what they are,' I asked,
'I know it's more than drifting drives you on,
or dodging the paternal bullet?' Tasked,
he ordered rum, sat mum a while, then yawned.
'You want an Atlas of the soul... Alask-
a links to Russia; Panama's a join;
the Horns are hinges to the Orient's door –
the Earth's a board game we can fold in four.

7
'The Chinese thought that Heaven rested here
at four fixed points upon their ancient map;
the Persians that four genies strained to bear
the upper realms – we know now that's all crap,
but still conceive in joinery, think we're
linked, that our economic quoins hold up
the whole world's roof, that nation speaks to nation
in Capital's one tongue without translation…

8
'Since Mercator unpeeled this fruitful globe
and set her segments out for all to gauge,
the Earth's four edge's mystique's been disrobed –
we realise the world is not a page;
but still we hope for pockets we can probe
for keys to open our omniscient cage,
so to the corners of the continents
we look for ingress to our lost intents.

9
'I wanted to cost human intimacy:
the price paid for its lack, not just the ghosts
of lust we're haunted by or hunt, their lacy
trace of love's spoor across the body's coasts
and hinterlands, but the intricacies
mind mints to trade between thought's guests, thoughts' host
negotiating where we do not know
the stakes, what closenesses are only show?'

10
I watched him strain his arms out wide as though
they'd reach around the earth and somehow touch;
next he bowed down until he clamped his jaw
upon his glass – half-crucified, half-crouched,
both charlatan and sacrifice – swallowed
a slug by snapping back in swift embouch –
and talked, as though I were his last acknowledger;
and talked, as though to amputate an onager.

11
And what he said is carried over here –
to versify is cutting through the truth
to find another verity: the sheer
edge of its grain, the fact as foot, and both
translations of each other, bere to beer
and beer as liquid bread: he said, 'To Youth!'
Our glasses clashed; I wrote, 'To Youth's departure.'
He lost himself to story, herein captured.

12
He said, 'I woke up in an iron bed
ringed by my public, in the attic room
of Love's Museum – rain's ecstatic threads
belaboured at the Stamboul glass. Entombed
in Orhan's Innocence, I lay unread
till closing time, then slunk into the gloom
of January, pausing at the shoppie
for a translation – but they had no copy.

13
'Climbing the hill past junk-shops, the hammam,
I met two pals who claimed they browsed for busts
of Ataturk, and moaned that I'd become
pseudo-Kemal, the Lazarus of lust,
that plague that feeds on neediness, shame's sham
dictator, who spontaneously combusts
the tinder hearts of rutting's sad obsessives,
those who in social grammar are possessives...'

14
'I have to be the Porlock to your Khan:
how did we get to Istanbul from – where
were we, exactly?' 'Broken up in Pan-
ama, alas – la Kuna on the tear.
We'll see that lachrymose lagoon again
before we have to leave this liars' lair...
first, after I woke up inside a book,
let's see the turn that Turkish evening took.

15
'We argued over love as a museum,
since letters can't preserve the flesh we've felt.
Lips' press on cigarette stubs are the dumb
flex of time's perineum. Organs melt
like soap, our photos ghost us, mausoleums
of glass hold raki relics – memory's pelt
hangs on the Sultan's wall to honour him,
and not the lover left without a limb.

16
'Another rakı off the Rue de Pera –
Ricardo, rancorous, declared Pamuk's
authorial hubris daunts mere pride – how dare he
erect a monument to his own book?
Vida took theoretic task: compare a
concept to a fiction: what's more worth a look?
I said I know where this can be resolved –
the Loser's Club, where reason is devolved.

17
'Istiklal's pavements cackled in the rain
as we resumed our scuttling to Taksim.
(This was before the riots – or between,
to be more accurate, since rights, it seems,
are always interim.) Now, in my brain
the route was clear, or rather, in my dreams –
though we searched sidestreets, asked in dim hotels,
the Loser's Club was washed away, like smells

18
'of cooking that would make your uncle cry…
The irony of losing it began
to make itself clear, as we failures dried
ourselves off in a tiny restaurant.
I hired an upstairs room – they fed the fire
with broken furniture, brought us scran
of Anatolia, ripped us off for whisky –
and we told tales about the lost grown frisky.

19
'The Losers' Club's no place that you can find
and still be called a member – you and Groucho
already knew this – it's that state of mind
that like a ghost dog tracks you, polter-pooch who
drunks meet in small hour streets and nameless wynds.
It is that table, knocking when you slouch to
slumber, as though you'd let in reason's monsters.
Revolvers are its chambers, Scotch its minster.

20
'Vida, fond of the Princes' Islands, ordered
first grilled sardines then macaronic Greek:
'Cruel Nísia ton Gatón, where purring borders
on noise pollution, mewers muse, and sleek
puss-pashas growl all songbirds must be murdered –
should the catch fail, they'd eat us in a week...
Let feathering wakes receive bread from our ferry:
farewell to felines, insular as worry!'

21
'Ricardo, thinking back to how we'd sprawled
like bream upon Çemerlitaş's slab,
its pepperpot dome overhead, recalled
how Sinan was caught idling on the job,
or so great Süleyman supposed, appalled
he'd gone to Hagia Sofia for a nap.
His architect replied, 'To best Justinian,
just listen to this silence of dominion.'

22
'What story did you tell?' '– Of Soutar Johnny,
who was, while Tam o' Shanter played his field
of fancies shaped like females, making money –
far likelier to cause gleg Kate to yield
than Tam's tall tale about his tail-less pony.
And so he haunted her, till she revealed
that instrument her husband used to play,
and taught him tunes while Tammas was away.'

23
He broke off suddenly, grinned and confessed,
'All this is an extended metaphor
for something or someone I must repress –
good faith, bad trade: it's what a symbol's for.
Some lovers find no profit in excess
while others claim that love itself breeds more:
Having been both, I will not quantify
love's quantum here – I know you want to pry.

24
'But power is atomised into each cell
in which we meet – behind a bedroom door
or in a judge's chambers: one compels,
if only the once; another must demur.
Pure continuity's craved by the self
more than sex, and, if granted, how we whore
ourselves to those who save us from the facts,
permitting us to live in *entr'acte*.

25
'We took the ferry back in early morning,
the Bosphorus a laminate of moon
scattered with daylight's roe; watched gulls' slow turning,
high in the interstitial air, balloons
of mosques still almost rising; stood, spurning
the cabin's warmth to stir with plastic spoons
the *sahlep*'s hot and cinnamony trance –
and think of sleep, its arrogant advance.

26
'Did I tell you the route to NovoTsargrad?'
he asked me suddenly, and I looked up:
his face was frozen over, crackled, haggard.
'We only met today.' 'That was some trip:
you might as well have crossed the bridge to Asgard –
no railway then, just boredom and the whip;
by tarantass, barouches, ferries, sleds,
a whaleship – to the Empire of the Dead!

27
'You won't find where we went in any atlas,
and I should know because I drew the map:
cryptocartography's my field, the subtlest
of military arts – we fooled the Japs
for years until *katana* came to cutlass.
Atlantis of the Arctic Circle slipped
beneath the pack ice, Dallas Borealis,
the Bering Straits' Byzantium, sunk by malice...'

28
'You're saying there's a second Istanbul
between Siberia and Alaska?' 'Was,
dear boy, for centuries – we couldn't fool
the weather or the waking world, alas,
past Revolution, but before that fall
into the post-imperial crevasse,
there was a city straddling the ice
where Greek was sung – a polar paradise.

29
'To get there, though, was Purgatory worse
than Dante clambered up – the mud
that jellied into boots; the stupid horse,
the lame one; skeeters suckling at your blood;
your fellow officers, those maddening bores,
bellowing re boots, horses, and bad food;
those sausages like dogs' tails dipped in tar;
then fish-faced bourgeois, brains like caviar –

30
'and everyone a writer – police inspectors,
the college registrar – their poems, plays
and novels bursting from their breeches – actors
sick for applause. One shadowed us for days:
pince-nez, a rusty cough, some Moscow doctor
who must reform our prisons – people say
what tosh they like out there, no fear of trouble...
a card-game helped relieve him of his roubles

31
'while waiting for the Baikal ferry, bored
out of our fishless, milkless, breadless brains –
who fetches while there's vodka? We ignored
the massive mirror of that sea, complained
competitively: best was first aboard,
and straight into the galley to explain,
'*Cher* chef, my kingdom for a chicken soup!'
Filthy plate, horse-stink – and delicious gloop.

32
'Halfway across you stare straight down a mile
as though you woke to find yourself mid-cloud.
The whole ship shuddered like a convict while
the hangman chats, and straightens out his shroud,
as though Leviathan gave us a smile
and rose to swallow up both meek and proud.
We hit the shore, took horse, and, lathering leather,
escaped the lake, its dreadful placid weather.

33
'The doctor/writer came with us to catch
the Amur ferry, though he couldn't stand
our boon companion, Schmidt, who liked to screech
his arias as we rode. When he complained,
the loud lieutenant said, 'Out here, we each
must be as liberal as we understand.'
This was the smartest thing that he'd professed,
and even passing beavers looked impressed.

34
'I fucked a Japanese professional
while comets filled the cabin or my head –
fireflies, although they didn't seem that small.
She did: I barely found her in my bed;
I steered by tits and tittering until
her fold of cotton wiped up what I'd shed.
As I admired the lacquer of her locks
we turned, and in the doorway sat a fox.

35
'From Khabarovsk we followed when the river
skewed north, as though it fled the failing sun;
and commandeered the boat in that endeavour,
quite disaffecting crew, whores, everyone –
Schmidt bearing arms would cause a bear to shiver
So, no love lost, the Amur our bad pun,
we left the hawthorn and the poplar's slopes
for sandbanks, then Sakhalin's lack of hope.

36
'From Khabarovsk we followed when the river
skewed north, as though it fled the failing sun;
and commandeered the boat in that endeavour,
quite disaffecting crew, whores, everyone –
Schmidt bearing arms would cause a bear to shiver
So, no love lost, the Amur our bad pun,
we left the hawthorn and the poplar's slopes
for sandbanks, then Sakhalin's lack of hope.

37
'I've drawn the island like a drowned girl's husk,
her profile stares at Russia, at her back
a roaring, ice-clogged sea, the raw Okhotsk.
We missed the last lighthouse, caught the smoke
a whaler's stack sent up into the dusk.
A filthy crossing almost saw us wrecked,
and then, upon the *Kelet*'s prow, an eagle
the captain had chained there: old Empire's sigil.

38
'We left the women – fair enough exchange:
convicts needs wives, and we required supplies.
Above the vast trench of the deep, estranged
from anywhere, with fishscales in our eyes,
we passed Kamchatka's sheer volcanic range –
calderas' spume and whale-steam equalised.
The wind appeared to skin us of our names,
but still the stink of blubber clung like shame.

39
'The captain's name, Atlasov, stuck with me
because this sea, he claimed, was only charted
on his brain's parchment – and his ancestry
included that brave Cossack who cavorted
down the peninsula on murderous sprees
till butchered in his bed. Each morning started
with his releasing of the eagle, who
then promptly caught a salmon both would chew.

40
'He didn't keep a log, and so we didn't know
how long it took to reach the whalebone walls
of NovoTsargrad: twenty feet high snow-
packed ribs they topped with giant greying skulls.
Chukotka warriors manned the checkpoints, so
we had to wait there for three days until
a *dragoumanos* came from Diomede,
the island where Vyronas has his seat.

41
'Chukotka like to tell cod tales, Atlasov
to mistranslate – we sat below the glow
of baleful bile auroras, rendered passive
by vodka and accounts of that freakshow
emperor: his girl-headed flies; his massive
sea-worms that cough up ships; the two
gold-tusked guard-walruses that flank his throne
astride the dateline; his own timeless zone.

42
'Vyronas was a demigod or despot,
though which precisely seemed to be unclear.
The Bering Straits were certainly his piss-pot:
each trapper, whaler, fisher owed his share,
and vassal tribes like theirs must live in cesspits
while he reclined on pelts of polar bear;
from *Avrio Anaktoron*, in quartz
and ice and ivory, he controlled their ports.

43
'Some said he fled Byzantium at the Fall,
while others claimed he'd led the ' 21 –
all knew him as white-armoured, mute-mouthed, tall
beyond all tribesmen, speaking to no-one
except his daughter, and invulnerable
to arrow or harpoon – they'd pinned him down
that last rebellion, shattered all their spears –
he'd fed their hearts to his eight-legged bears.

44
'His daughter, Ada, famously, would ride
to take the census on a mammoth's back;
her quick wits saw her ruling at his side,
her saga on his reign was just the facts
in fifteen vol.s; she swam against the tide
two miles to warn him of the Yanks' attack –
I wondered as we finally retired
what further gifts of hers I might admire?

45
'They'd lock us in a concrete lookout tower –
though where we'd go they knew we'd no idea.
The curtains rustled as in Ada's bower –
except there were no curtains: what we'd hear
were cockroach colloquies and bugs in showers,
pouring through ceiling cracks to crawl in ears
and sleeves and boots. Hôtel Splendide it wasn't -
each morning we awoke bamboozled, dozent.

46
'Remember how those Norse gods – Loki, Thor –
on reaching Jotunheim, put themselves up
in an abandoned mead-hall hung with fur,
sharing its bedroom, girning at this slap
in the face – no-one feasting them – before
they recognised the hall where they had slept:
a giant's mitt. And so we passed the night,
awaiting Hermes in the dawn's lame light.'

47
And as he finished dawn was rolling in
to fill the valleys eastward to the sea.
We ordered coffee, watched a dorsal fin
of mist roll over in the rising heat
through caffeinated steam. Where to begin?
'Did you and this Vyronas ever meet?
Was he the poet?' 'Who?' 'Is this a ploy?
How did Byzantium become Dalstroy?'

48
'I met a poet once in Africa...'
'I have to know: how did that radical
of morals and poetics...please, what flaw
metamorphoses Byron..."What dye call
him?' '...into Berzin?' 'Him I did once know –
ironically in Philly. I recall
that loveless *bratka* browsing gramophones –
the greedy troll-king played Grieg to his drones.'

49
'But back to Africa, upon the Horn...'
– And so he'd leap; impossible to steer
away from veering, as befits one born
to variation; schooled by bitter years
in deft digression, he had come to scorn
frankness the way a vintner would scorn beer.
Put plainly, good plain English was obtuse:
for any muse but fog he had no use.

50
'I was with Burton down in Berbera
when Speke was spiked eleven times and lived –
he didn't talk about it much, whereas
Ricardo would orate in volumes vivid
as that Somali spear that pierced his jaw
on themes like Harar's emir who perceived
the glint of British greed behind his pose –
which was why Rimbaud liked me, I suppose.'

51
'Really. Where was this?' 'Aden, probably,
Perhaps *Le Grand Hotel de l'Univers* –
the heat is not an aid to memory.'
'And you ran guns?' 'Well, I was barely there,
too stoned to be particular, while he...
with him you'd never know, you'd just infer.
He never spoke, or far too much, as though
words were another way of saying no.

52
'You must have known your cargo.' 'We'd spend weeks,
months, in some port that was a dozen shacks,
a score of *akal*s made of rags and sticks,
awaiting papers, paying bakshish, 'tax';
our goods stacked in the shade where shady Greeks
appended theirs. You can't prepare, relax –
'*L'air de Djibouti égare les sens...*' Time crazes,
And things take *longtemps* in these filthy places.

53
'Eventually you leave before the dawn –
a hundred camels and a hundred men,
a legion entering the burnt place on
an instinct passing commerce: to depend
on no man's system. Rest each afternoon,
then march till, kraaled in dark, your last defence
is what the camels sense: they'll chew the cud,
then stop and point, then piss themselves with dread.

54
'Somalis milk a camel reaching up
so juggle with their milk-jug and one knee –
a sort of yoga pose to fill your cup.
Each supper was a slap of rice and ghee;
his silence by the fireside – up he'd hop,
and off: don't think I ever saw him sleep.
Each morning there he'd stomp, the most awake,
left shoulder leading, hauling in his wake

55

'the whole shebang of dromedaries, goods,
clansmen, armed Abyssinians, unarmed mules,
and even me, poor drochle of the brood
of Donna Ines, in his shoes, the soles
of which, of Afar make, were heeled and toed
the same way, suitable, he said, for fools
like us, who don't know if we come or go
avec semelles de vent on sand or snow.

56

'Those times that terrify the most – our deaths
(our own, our others' – those our love must claim) –
burn out time's circuitry: are space, have depth.
The consciousness imagines it must calm
the panicked animal it's cabined with,
but then it rescues us, poor surly camel,
and carries us across that frightening place
like nomads. I could see it in his face,

57

'how Rimbaud was compelled to seek it out,
to burn and scatter pages of the self,
rinçures of reason: genius was a lout
to be precise, desire an empty shelf –
you align the inner and the outer gulf
by ledger, rifle, *gaflah*; be the scout
of barrenness, the *abban* to the void.
Chew *qat*, trade coffee, try to stay employed.

58
'Then we Shadrached into the shadeless zone
and the breath of the furnace baked our faces,
and we Meshached among the mountains, cones
like robes of Sufis whirling in the graces
of God, until we were Abed-Negone –
at which point someone shimmered in the blaze's
distance, approaching like a fiery stroller,
his arms draped from the stick across his shoulders.

59
'This was some herdsman Rimbaud seemed to know
and trust enough to halt the caravan –
'A poet, so he says, though they all do,'
was all he'd say, and then a marathon
of trotting over glitter, squeezing through
thorn-gulches, following our paragon
of silence into valleys draped with burqas
of evening shade – less hike and more mazurka.

60
'Until we halted at a giant bell,
a *Tsarsky Kolokol* of solid rock
to summon Ozymandias from Hell,
and on the flanks of this huge egg, this cloche,
were paintings, ancient as the stone itself
or so they seemed out here, before all clocks:
giraffes, an elephant, a lucid fever
of colour, and, *une liberté plus libre*,

61

'banner-large cattle, men with arms flung wide,
and on the next rock and the next, arms splayed,
ecstatic figures – 'The Uncrucified',
he called them, following this long parade
and laughing for the first time. By their side
his self-sewn sails of clothing, dust-caked, frayed,
were of a piece. The herdsman tapped his pole,
'No camels, look: before we need a soul.'

62

'I caught a fever then for real, from where
who knew? – just God's small notice He was out.
They rigged a litter up, paid four to bear
me for a thaler each. (I'm too kaput
to bargain, seeing things, part-child, part-hare,
that walk beside me, flinching when I shout.)
And thus I crossed the great Rift Valley, climbed
into the highlands, raving, self-beslimed.

63

'We sat in Harar at that journey's end,
the city's wall enclosing like the hull
of night's high ark, and heard hyenas rend
meat market scraps. He mentioned how he'd culled
two thousand dogs with strychnine, how his friends –
the Europeans – laughed, but were appalled.
'I'm Abdo Rinbo now', he deadpan-muttered,
and from those eyes my own stared back, anothered.

64
'Which brings me back by circumjackery
to Darien, asylum of the Scots...'
I took this for a try at waggery,
or else as proof that he had lost all plots;
his vanity would stun a Thackeray,
but this was a Flash Gordian of knots.
'You can't get there from Harar!' I exclaimed.
He eyed me sharply, laughed, and then explained:

65
'If Harar was a ship, its captain was
the Ras, soon father of the emperor,
Tafari, in whose cabin I, because
of shipwreck, was nicknamed *Naufragio*, or
'The Drowned'; while Rimbaud, rebel for applause,
played Long John Silver, tucking a twelve bore
into his oxter, claiming those who'd sailed
on Scottish vessels were aquatic Gaels.

66
'And so, when I, washed-up, was washed up on
Isla Ballena, crannog to the Kuna,
Darien, gyte colony of slow despond
for Scotland, lay nearby. The village *junta*,
hearing in their long house of my sick bond
with hubris and with greed, decreed the *Punta
Escoces* might be visited, so I
could pay respects to Death before I die.

67
'Before that, though, I tried to build up strength
by pacing round the tiny central square
where, with a large mock turtle for a plinth,
a guid Scots cannon sat, as though to scare
the *waga* jaguars away. At length
the girls emerged to watch, with cropped black hair
and *mola* blouses, each brocaded with
birds, superheroes, healing plants and myths.

68
'An elder sold me a machete – showed
me how, by notching it into bamboo,
you file it fit for Occam; helped me load
the *cayuco*, then listed terrors to
avoid: tarantulas, palm vipers, toads, the goad
of red fire-ants, sand-flies... As we paddled through
the excremental halo round the island,
his list went on – my heart was in the highlands

69
'or lowlands, Govan – anywhere but here...
Again with the translucence: leopard rays
pacing a coral Alhambra's corridor.
Then, at the inlet's entrance, something raised
a three foot fin, U-Boating out before
we scraped our way in over living blades –
And suddenly the jungle was about
our barque: its stink, its silent sullen glut

70
'broken by capuchins' high chittery chat –
the Elder Tomas, expert in distress,
said, 'Monkey like to cack upon your hat.'
I peered up into clammy gloom, impressed
that they could see to aim; glimpsed fruit-bats
like foxes hung in sacks. I sniffed the cess
of mangrove, brackish pools, rainforest floor,
and, wobbling wildly, tried to step ashore.

71
'There was, of course, of Nuevo Edinburgh,
no trace. The jungle, like an anaconda,
swallowed it whole. A few spars, like a curragh,
showed where 'The Olive Branch' had sunk, gone under
without a shot – a cooper in a hurry
for the drink took a candle, and... no wonder,
trapped between bad luck, the flux ,and Spain,
two thousand Scots should fail to call this 'hame'.

72
'We found earthworks, belt-buckles, and the well
the last defenders dug behind their ditch –
no bones: oblivion's boa ate those as well.
Queen Anne would recompense the rich;
the Equivalent Society would swell
into the Royal Bank, or, England's Bitch.
Meanwhile, brown pelicans flop out to sea,
and white-lipped peccaries rush through the trees.

73
'I classified the last, to keep me calm:
cedro espina, a giant, centuries old;
swamp apple, *bombacopsis,* prickle palm;
the candle-tree… then Tomas stopped me, told
the story of his Kuna Blanco dream:
how searching in the mountain streams for gold
he'd found plantations growing peppers, maize,
pineapples, yams, just like in ancient days.

74
'The people farming there invited him
to feast with them, and all their tables creaked
like ships at sea with fresh-caught fish, roast game –
and then he sees that they are white, and speak
in English, but their faces are the same
as his grandparents in their youth, just bleached
like bones, and grainy like old photographs:
they tell him that he's dreaming, and they laugh,

75
'which wakes him – then he laughs because it's true.
We think our dreams are spirits, so we find
they're angry with us, that we can't see through
their veil into the world. So he's some kind
of glorious unmute Hume who'd have me throw
my demons out by chewing on some vine –
I puked my visions up with Castaneda,
besides, it's evening, and we can see *nada*.'

76
And it was evening in Caracas too.
Somehow we were in some *heladería*,
though how we'd got there, as he'd say, who knew?
Through barrios and barricades' hysteria,
oblivious or ghosts ourselves by now,
we'd walked and talked our way to Altamira.
Perhaps wherever he was, was the eye
of some tornado of the psyche – why,

77
I'd no more time to ponder: years, it seemed,
had passed since we first met, and I felt tired
beyond whatever weariness could mean.
I left him sitting there to be admired
anew, still talking, chomping on ice cream –
turrón, the flavor of his youth's desires.
His words, that proved more intimate than kisses,
already drew the scorn of cool-eyed misses:

78
'Darien in darkness is where failure meets
its own: poor Fergusson in piss-straw hell;
or on Point Look Out's battlements, John Keats,
his silence a Constantinople's fall.
Unwritten books are like revised defeats;
burnt libraries reform in small hours' pall.
The bay fills with a legion of such ghosts,
all rotting fiercely as the Scots' house posts.

79
'With insect hymnals printed on our bones,
we woke to find our kit of interest
to Don Agouti, and breakfast not our own,
according to the millipedes. There passed
an hour of turquoise butterflies, who shone
and shimmered up a canal headed west –
cut through the coral, narrow as a pend –
I tracked it for miles, but never found an end...'

Little Red Robot (Hidden Track)

for Paul Summers

The Herd Groyne Light at South Shields was, unbeknownst to strangers, a late Victorian automaton made out of cast iron and corrugated steel that had, mid-bellow on its foghorn in the early 1960s, become self-aware.

The Little Red Robot had no arms, so, when it strutted round the docks and former shipyards on its three red legs it had to pretend it had its hands behind its back like a time and motion inspector.

Every now and then it would stride to the end of the pier and look out at the container ships crossing the bar. It supposed these contained spare parts for all the lighthouses of these islands - reflectors and bulbs and panes and frames and self-assembly kits, so that every route might be safely illumined.

It imagined that they contained all the sunken ships ever recovered or yet to be recovered, including those known only by sonar or submarine cameras as wielded by, it supposed, tiny submersible versions of itself, together with their drowned crews, properly readied for burial, and all their cargoes, whether tinned hams, stacked Willow Pattern porcelains, or ancient amphorae of, still, perfectly drinkable wine.

This made it so excited it could not contain itself, and it would squat and lay a red phone box or, sometimes, a scarlet pillar box.

As one of these was almost as outmoded as the other, police helicopters would come and chase it away, and council refuse trucks would set up a perimeter while they cleaned the mess.

Occasionally, however, local people, who knew to look out for such incidents as their ancestors might have kept an eye out for wrecks, would post love letters, or attempt to make calls before the phone boxes could be shut down.

The authorities were legally obliged to honour these attempts at communication. But, to their bewilderment, they found they were mostly addressed to former regimes, fabulous entities, or, simply, the dead.

It wasn't clear whether this was a marvellous coincidence, or something people felt compelled to enact – or if this was some metamorphosing power of the Little Red Robot itself.

Whichever, whether the letters were addressed to ordinary workers in the former Soviet Union, to Red Skelton or the Scarlet Woman of Revelations, or were recorded messages to dead aunts or ex-lovers, every effort was made to deliver such communications, even if this amounted to an official impersonating the intended addressee and forging their reply.

When this happened, the Little Red Robot felt like its imaginary arms had extended so far as to embrace the entire world!

Acknowledgements

'Afterself' was published in *Discourses: Poems for the Royal Institution*, ed. Jo Shapcott (The Royal Institution in association with the Calouste Gulbenkian Foundation, 2002).

'On Your Nerve (A Wake for Frank O'Hara)' was performed by WN Herbert, David Kinloch, and Donny O'Rourke in the CCA, Glasgow, and other venues in 1996, and published in *Verse*, vol.14, no.1, ed. Brian Henry, Nancy Schoenberg, and Andrew Zawacki (1997).

Poems from 'Homage to the Anxious City' formed part of *Flying Homages*, performed by Julia Darling, Linda France, WN Herbert, and Colin Teavon at Northern Stage in 2004.

'The Working Self' was published in *Contemporary Poetry and Contemporary Science*, ed. Robert Crawford (OUP, 2005).

'neareast' was published in *A Balkan Exchange: Eight Poets from Bulgarian and Britain*, ed. WN Herbert (Arc Publications in association with New Writing North, 2007).

'Revenant' was published in *Signs and Humours*, ed. Lavinia Greenlaw (Calouste Gulbenkian Foundation, 2007).

The pamphlet *Murder Bear* was published by Donut Press in 2013.

The libretto 'Little Instruments of Apprehension', devised with composer Evangelia Rigaki and choreographer Darren Ellis, was performed at the Tête-à-Tête Festival in 2009.

'Don Juan's Pilgrimage' was published in *A Modern Don Juan: Cantos for These Times by Divers Hands*, ed. Andy Croft and Nigel Thompson (Five Leaves, 2014).